near Bristol & Bath

Nigel Vile

COUNTRYSIDE BOOKS
NEWBURY BERKSHIRE

First Published 2007

COUNTRYSIDE BOOKS
3 Catherine Road
Newbury, Berkshire

To view our complete range of books,
please visit us at
www.countrysidebooks.co.uk

ISBN 978 1 84674 014 5

Photographs by the author
Cover picture shows the view from Blagdon Hill

Designed by Peter Davies, Nautilus Design
Produced through MRM Associates Ltd, Reading
Printed by Borcombe Printers plc, Romsey

Contents

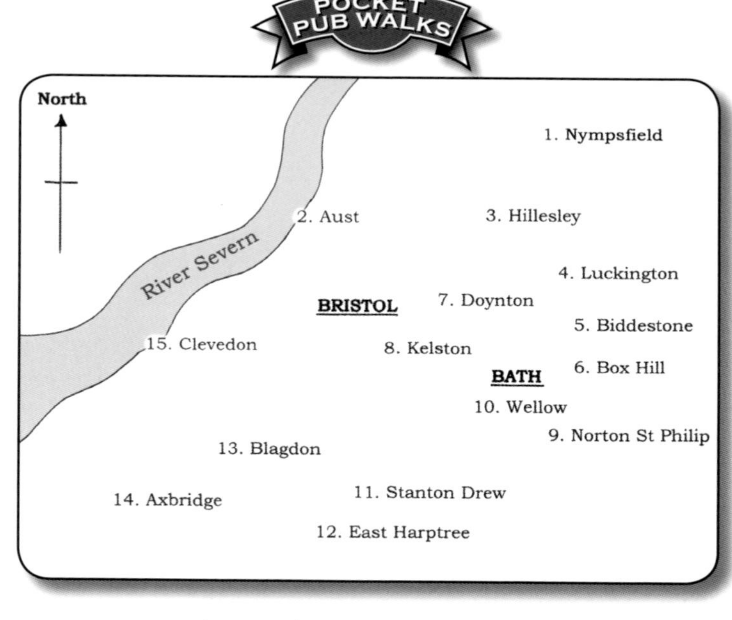

Area map showing location of the walks

Introduction

What better way to spend a leisurely few hours than to stretch your legs and then visit a traditional pub for a delicious meal or snack and a glass of beer or wine? The 15 circular walks in this book allow you to do just that. Each route – that includes, or is just a short drive from, a recommended pub – takes you through some of the finest scenery in the Bath and Bristol area.

The variety of landscape types in this part of the country is both rich and diverse. To the west of these great cities we have the Severn Estuary and the Bristol Channel, where the visitor can enjoy far-ranging and expansive views, and where the extensive mud flats at low tide make for an ornithologist's paradise. Inland from the Severn lie the Cotswold Hills, where the honey-coloured cottages and picture-postcard villages maintain their endless appeal for tourists from far and wide. To the south of Bath and Bristol the limestone creates the rather more rugged and dour landscape of the Mendip Hills. Here are some of the more strenuous walks in the region, with the hilltops nudging that seemingly magical 1,000 ft contour line.

There is also a rich array of features that reflect the imprint of human settlement. Woodchester, for example, is a delightful estate created in a dramatic Cotswold valley, whilst at Clevedon is the town's pier, which was much loved by John Betjeman amongst many others. Venture further south, to Blagdon, and there you will see the vast reservoirs of the Chew Valley, whilst at Axbridge can be found King John's Hunting Lodge, a modern creation compared to the ancient stone circle at Stanton Drew. The list of highlights seems almost endless!

The walks are between three and seven miles in length. Car parking options in the vicinity of each pub have been suggested, although in many cases it will be possible to park at the hostelry itself. In such cases, you must seek the landlord's permission first in case parking is at a premium, and promise to return for a meal and a drink. A sketch map indicating the route to be followed accompanies each walk. However, I would always recommend carrying the relevant OS Explorer or Outdoor Leisure map as well – these are as vital a part of the walker's kit as sturdy boots and a rucksack. The appropriate sheet number is given at the start of each walk.

To make your day complete, don't forget to carry a snack and a drink in that trusty rucksack, as well as a decent set of waterproofs – despite occasional belief to the contrary, authors of walking guidebooks cannot guarantee their readers sunny weather!

Nigel Vile

Publisher's Note

We hope that you obtain considerable enjoyment from this book; great care has been taken in its preparation. However, changes of landlord and actual closures are sadly not uncommon. Likewise, although at the time of publication all routes followed public rights of way or permitted paths, diversion orders can be made and permissions withdrawn.

We cannot, of course, be held responsible for such diversion orders and any inaccuracies in the text which result from these or any other changes to the routes nor any damage which might result from walkers trespassing on private property. We are anxious though that all details covering the walks and pubs are kept up to date and would therefore welcome information from readers which would be relevant to future editions.

The simple sketch maps that accompany the walks in this book are based on notes made by the author whilst checking out the routes on the ground. However, for the benefit of a proper map, we do recommend that you purchase the relevant Ordnance Survey sheet covering your walk. The Ordnance Survey maps are widely available, especially through booksellers and local newsagents.

1 Nympsfield

The Rose & Crown

For many years, the local news media had made references to the forgotten estate in the Cotswolds called Woodchester. In the depths of a secluded valley lay a crumbling mansion, surrounded by mature woodland and overgrown ponds. Then, in 1994, the estate passed into the hands of the National Trust, who set about protecting and preserving this unique landscape. Today's visitor will see the remains of an 18th- and 19th-century landscaped park, a mansion, and a chain of five lakes fringed by woodland and pasture. On this particular circuit of the park, there is much to catch the eye. As well as the mature woodland with the occasional viewpoint, the walk passes an ice house and ponds, a boathouse, the estate's quarry, and the mansion

Distance 3½ miles

OS Explorer 168 Stroud, Tetbury and Malmesbury. GR 799014.

Wooded hillsides and a flat valley bottom

Starting point The National Trust Woodchester Estate car park.

How to get there *4 miles north of Dursley, leave the B4066 Stroud road and follow the unclassified road signed to Woodchester and Nympsfield. In 300 yards, a left turn leads to the Woodchester estate car park. On returning to the unclassified road, turn left and it is just ½ mile to Nympsfield and the Rose and Crown.*

itself. Herein lies a tale of mystery and intrigue. William Leigh, a 19th-century ship owner from Liverpool, bought the estate in 1845 and demolished the old house. Work on a new Victorian mansion began but was abandoned after sixteen years, leaving a fascinating, unfinished Gothic building!

THE PUB

The **Rose & Crown** is a 400-year-old former coaching inn, lovingly crafted from the warm honey-coloured stone that typifies the Cotswold Hills. Internally, with natural stone and wood panelling, ancient beams, and open fires, there is a real traditional feel to this welcoming hostelry. The food is quite excellent, and ranges from sandwiches, baguettes, and jacket potatoes to unusual and imaginative restaurant-style meals. There is local cider and a good choice of wine, but a visit to the Rose and Crown would be incomplete without a pint of Old Spot from the Uley Brewery nearby. To quote the strapline, this is 'inn keeping with tradition'.

Opening hours are 11 am to 11 pm; Sunday, noon to 10.30 pm.
☎ *01453 860240*

1 Descend some steps from the car park down to a woodland track; turn right and, at a junction in 250 yards, turn left to follow the waymarked **Woodland Walk** (blue arrows). Follow the woodland path uphill to a viewpoint, passing **Marmontsflat quarry**. Beyond the viewpoint, continue following the **Woodland Walk** as it winds its way downhill to a junction, with a track in the valley bottom.

2 This track is part of the **Boathouse Walk** marked with orange arrows. Follow this track to the left for 350 yards to the next significant junction, turn left and follow a path that runs through the valley bottom above **Brick Kiln Pond**. At a junction, where the red '**Valley Walk**' forks left uphill, continue through the valley bottom for 100 yards to a junction. Turn right – following the orange waymarks – and, in 40 yards, turn left to follow the **Boathouse Walk** to the far end of **Middle Pond**.

3 Turn right, cross the dam at the eastern end of **Middle Pond** and, once across the water, pass through a gate on the right into

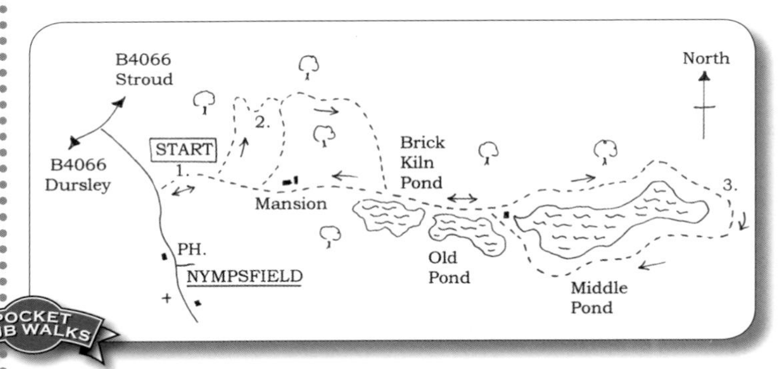

Middle Pond passed at point 3 of the route.

a hillside field. Follow the path across this field to a hand gate, enter woodland and follow a path along the southern end of **Middle Pond** to some steps at its western end. Climb these steps, turn right and follow a path above the boathouse that soon bears left to run above **Old Pond**. Follow this path to some steps and a junction with a track. Turn left and follow this broad track through the valley bottom for 600 yards to the mansion. Continue for another ½ mile back to some steps and the car park.

Place of interest nearby

The **Museum in the Park** at Stratford Park near Stroud celebrates the rich history and heritage of the Stroud district. The 5,000 objects on display range from dolls and lawn mowers to flint arrowheads and bicycles. ☎ 01453 763394 or visit the museum's website on www.stroud.gov.uk/museum.

2 Aust

The Boar's Head

Before there were the Severn Railway tunnel and the Severn bridges, a simple ferry crossed the treacherous tidal waters of the river's vast estuary to Wales. At that time, the village of Aust had an importance far above its size. It was the last settlement before the ferry point, an important place for lodging and refreshment. There were many inns in what was a staging post on the journey west, but the passage of time has seen their number reduced to just one, the Boar's Head. As for the lane that led down to the ferry, today it is simply a cul-de-sac, severed by the M48 motorway. From the village, a complex network of field paths is followed as far as neighbouring Northwick, before the walk picks up the banks of the mighty Severn itself. River estuaries may be something of an acquired taste, but there is no doubting the magical atmosphere of the big skies and the mud

Distance 6 miles

OS Explorer 154 Bath and Bristol. GR 574890.

Flat field tracks and riverside paths; potentially muddy after rain

Starting point The Boar's Head pub in Aust village

How to get there *Leave the M48 just before the Severn road bridge and follow the A403 towards Avonmouth. In just 300 yards, turn left into Aust village, and in a further 300 yards park in the vicinity of a crossroads by the Evangelical church, just before the Boar's Head.*

flats, the open vistas and the flocks of wildfowl – a living Peter Scott canvas.

THE PUB

The **Boar's Head** is an attractive ivy-clad hostelry, with a relaxed and leisurely atmosphere that stands in complete contrast to the hustle and bustle of traffic on the nearby motorway network. With a series of linked rooms and alcoves, and beams and exposed stonework, there is a real traditional feel to the place, too. As well as prepared wraps and jacket potatoes, omelettes and ciabatta sandwiches, customers can enjoy a selection of excellent daily specials from the main menu. Local ales are also available, including brews from Abbey Ales in Bath. For those sunny weekend lunchtimes, there is also a most attractive garden with lawns.

Opening hours are noon to 3 pm and 6 pm to 11 pm; Sunday, noon to 3 pm and 7 pm to 10.30 pm.
☎ *01454 632278*

1 At the crossroads by the **Evangelical church**, follow the green lane that heads out of **Aust** in a southerly direction, opposite **Sandy Lane**. In ½ mile, where the enclosed track ends, continue for 100 yards along the right edge of an open field, with a drainage ditch called **Foss Ditch** to the right, to a gate on the right. Walk diagonally across the next field to a gate in its far corner and, in the following field, head across to a footbridge in the opposite boundary. Beyond this bridge, head for a stile in the far right-hand corner of the following field. Then follow the right edge of the next two small fields, crossing footbridges over

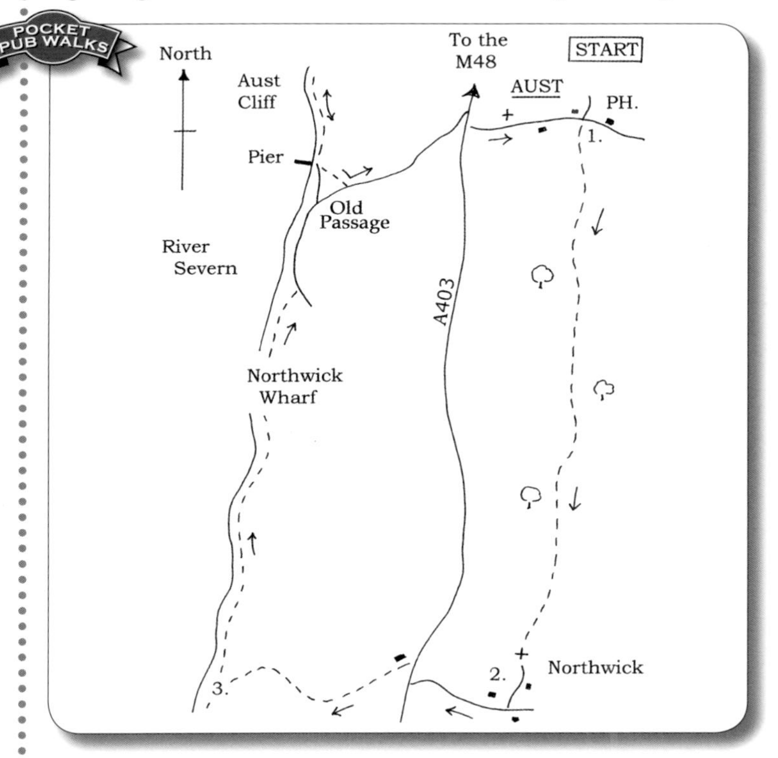

drainage ditches along the way. Beyond the footbridge at the far side of the second field, cross to yet another footbridge, some 150 yards ahead, before walking straight across the next field to an old gateway in the opposite boundary. Follow the right edge of the next field to a hand gate and a track. Cross the track to a stile opposite, and continue along the left edge of the field ahead to a stile in the far-left corner and **Northwick church**.

2 Walk across the churchyard to a gate, and continue along a back lane to the B4055. Turn right here and walk for 200 yards to the junction with the A403. Turn right and, in 20 yards, cross the main road to a stile opposite, just to the left of a drive leading to **Greenfield Farm**. Cross this stile, follow the right edge of the field ahead to a gateway. Just beyond the gateway, cross a stile on the right and turn left to follow a short section of enclosed path into a paddock. Walk the length of the paddock to a stile in the far right corner and, in the next field, follow the left-hand field boundary down to a footbridge. Cross this and bear left to a stile in the corner of the field. In the next field bear half right to an old gateway halfway along the right-hand boundary and join the embankment that borders the **Severn**.

3 Turn right and follow the embankment (which serves as a flood defence) for 1 mile, to a quiet lane. Follow the lane to the left – it borders the **Severn** – for ½ mile, to **Old Passage**. At a junction just before a hill leading past some large properties, turn left along the cul-de-sac that leads to the derelict **Severn** ferry building and pier. Now comes a short and rewarding detour (to avoid the detour, simply turn right at this point): continue along the concrete path by the old ferry building towards the first **Severn** bridge. As well as providing a fine view of the bridge, this path leads to **Aust Cliff**, a fossil hunter's paradise. Retrace your steps and go left along the path leading uphill to the road by **Old Passage House**, continuing for ½ mile to the junction with the A403. Opposite, slightly to the right, is the lane leading back into **Aust**.

The first Severn crossing viewed from the walk.

Place of interest nearby

The **Severn Bridge Visitors' Centre** at nearby Severn Beach has a wonderful exhibition showing the history of the River Severn crossings. Using interactive displays with video films, pictures, models, and descriptions of past and present crossings, the story of one of Britain's great feats of engineering is really brought to life. The centre is open from 11 am to 4 pm, Tuesday to Sunday, from Easter bank holiday weekend to late autumn. ☎ 01454 633511 for further information.

3 Hillesley

The Fleece Inn

Many Cotswold guidebooks appear to come no further south than Cirencester; it is almost as if that part of the Cotswolds consigned to South Gloucestershire were some other geographical entity! This walk will certainly dispel that myth. From Hillesley, where the Fleece Inn is a reminder of the source of wealth of the region in earlier times, field paths and tracks follow the Cotswold Edge to Hawkesbury and Hawkesbury Upton. The Cotswold Edge is the local term for that part of the Cotswolds where the escarpment drops steeply downhill to the Severn Vale. The views are correspondingly far-ranging, extending across the great river towards the Forest of Dean and the distant Welsh Hills. Beyond Hawkesbury Upton, the route descends into the Kilcott Valley, an archetypal slice of Cotswold landscape. Steep hillsides border a valley bottom watered by a sparkling stream, with handsome stone properties and farmsteads adding

Distance 6½ miles

OS Explorer 167 Thornbury, Dursley and Yate. GR 779897.

Hillsides and valleys in and around the Cotswold escarpment.

Starting point Kilcott Road in Hillesley, less than a minute's walk from the Fleece Inn.

How to get there *Leave the A46 at Dunkirk, 5 miles north of Old Sodbury, and follow the unclassified road leading to Hawkesbury Upton. Drive through the village and continue for another 1½ miles into Hillesley. Having passed Chapel Lane and the Fleece Inn on the right, turn into the next road on the right, Kilcott Road, and park with consideration on the roadside.*

an element of man-made interest at every turn. This is a circuit with just about everything the walker could hope for – fine cottages and grand houses, ancient churches, plunging valleys, woodland paths ... and a fine hostelry.

THE PUB

A black-and-white building – white plaster rendering and black paintwork – with a fine Cotswold stone roof, the **Fleece Inn** is a reminder of the cloth trade in the Cotswold Hills. The bar areas exude a sense of tradition and history, the dark wooden beams, hanging tankards, prints, and open log fire combining to produce a warm and welcoming feel. The extensive menu ranges from soup and breaded Brie wedges to wild mushroom strudel and poached fillet of salmon. Fine real ales are always available, too, including Butcombe and Black Sheep, as well as an ever-changing guest beer.

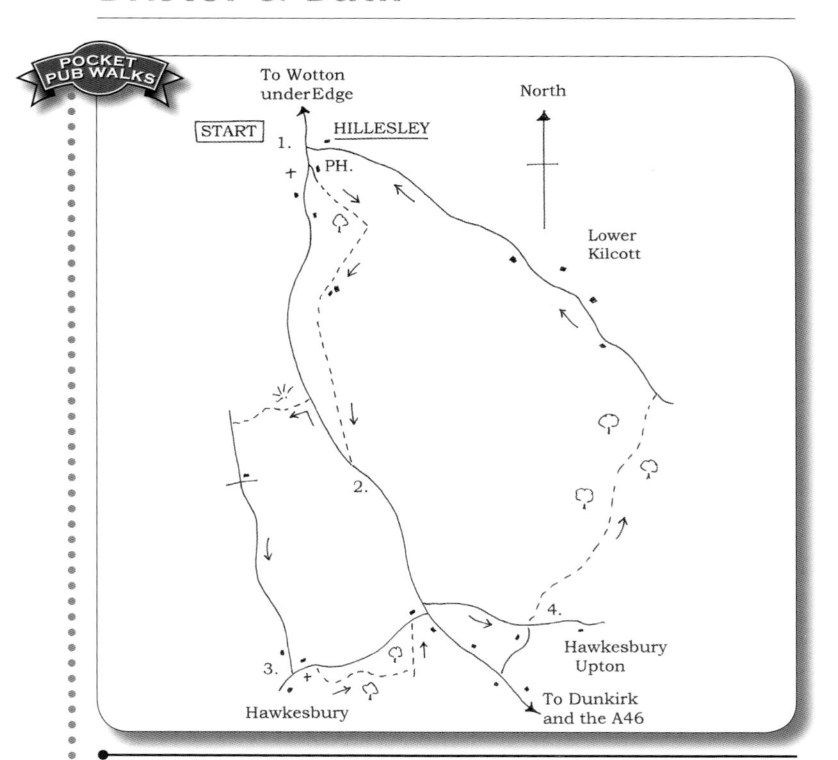

Opening hours are 11.30 am to 2.30 pm and 6 pm to 11pm; Sunday, noon to 3 pm and 6 pm to 10.30 pm.
☎ *01453 843189; website: www.thefleecehillesley.co.uk*

1 Return to the main road, turn left and then left again, into **Chapel Lane**, walking past the **Fleece Inn** to **Albany Cottage** at the top of the lane. Follow the track to the right of this property to a stile, and follow the left edge of the field ahead to a gate in the top left corner. Through the gate, follow an enclosed path uphill towards **Mear's Plantation**. Follow the main path directly uphill

through the woodland, ignoring an early path going off on the left. At the top of the climb, pass through a gateway and enter the corner of a field. Keep ahead for 20 yards, turn right through an old gateway, and continue along a grassy strip for ¼ mile to a stile in a fence just before a pair of buildings. Having passed the second property, **Splatt's Barn**, follow the drive to the left and continue along an unmetalled road for ½ mile to reach the **Hawkesbury** to **Hillesley** road.

2 Turn right, and follow this road for 300 yards until it bears right and drops downhill. At this point, pass through a gate on the left to join a waymarked path. Walk ahead for 20 yards until you see a hand gate on the left. Ignoring this gate, keep ahead for a further 10 yards to reach a second hand gate on the left. Pass through this gateway, turn right, and follow the hedgerow on the right downhill for 300 yards to a stile on the right. Cross this stile and one a few feet ahead; then cross the field beyond to a stile in the hedgerow opposite and turn left in the lane. Continue along the lane for 250 yards to a crossroads and follow the gated byway opposite. Follow this unmetalled road for ½ mile across open grassland to a gate and the lane in **Hawkesbury**.

Hillesley village.

3 Turn left, walk up the road that passes the church, and, in another 100 yards, veer right onto a path and climb uphill into some woodland. At the top of the woodland, beyond a gate, bear half left to reach a stile in the opposite hedgerow. Beyond the stile, follow the left-hand edge of the next two fields up to the **Cotswold Way**, at this point a broad track. Follow the track to the left for 300 yards to a lane, turn right, and follow the road in front of **Home Farm** and to the left of the drover's pool to reach the next junction. Turn left and, in 25 yards, turn right into **Starveall Lane**. Follow the lane for ½ mile to a junction, and take the footpath on the left.

4 Follow the path down a track to a stile; ahead is a valley. Follow a field path downhill across four fields along the valley, passing through gates at the end of each field. At the far end of the fourth field, beyond a gate, follow the path as it bears left into an area of woodland. Continue for 350 yards along the ride ahead – a stream over on the right – to a major junction of paths. Keep right and continue to follow a path running through the valley bottom for 600 yards to a stile and the lane in the **Kilcott valley**. Turn left and follow **Kilcott Road** for 1¼ miles back into **Hillesley**, ignoring all right and left turns along the way.

Place of interest nearby

The attractive market town of **Wotton-under-Edge** lies just a few miles north of Hillesley. There are no museums or galleries to visit, but Wotton has been accredited with the status of a 'Fair Trade town'. This makes for an interesting array of small independent retailers along its High Street. It is also worth seeking out the almshouses in Church Street, with their own diminutive chapel. For further information, contact Wotton's Heritage Centre on ☎ 01453 521541 or visit www.wottonheritage.com.

4 Luckington

The Old Royal Ship Inn

Mention the Cotswolds and names such as Stow-on-the-Wold, Painswick, and Broadway spring to mind. The Cotswold guidebook I have in front of me refuses to acknowledge anything south of Cirencester, for example. This delightful stretch of stony countryside, defined by the bedrock of oolitic limestone, clearly extends towards the fringes of both Bath and Bristol, where we find villages with that distinctive Cotswold feel. Luckington, Sherston and Brook End all possess that distinct character, with their picture-postcard cottages and churches, their tilestone roofing slabs and drystone walls. At its centre Luckington has a pleasant village green, while Sherston, whose signs proclaim 'England's oldest borough', was a traditional market centre with a broad main street. Brook End is a collection of cottages located alongside a ford that made national headlines in 2006. With the closure of the nearby B4040, satellite navigation systems were directing vehicles into some rather deep water with predictable consequences! The landscape hereabouts is dominated by the infant River Avon and its tributaries, a complex of shallow valleys and sparkling watercourses. Altogether, this is a delightful country walk on the Cotswold fringe.

THE PUB

The **Old Royal Ship Inn,** dating from the 17th century, enjoys an enviable location opposite the village green in Luckington. The traditional interior includes exposed stonework, an open fire, bare boards, and an array of complementary furnishings. With a menu that extends from sandwiches to fish, steak and poultry dishes, and real ales from Archers and Wadworth, there is something on offer to suit all tastes at this popular and welcoming hostelry.

Opening hours are 11.30 am to 2.30 pm and 6 pm to 11 pm; Saturday, 11 am to 11 pm; Sunday, noon to 10.30 pm.
☎ *01666 840222*

Distance 4½ miles

OS Explorer 168 Stroud, Tetbury and Malmesbury. GR 832840.

A gently undulating landscape

Starting point The village green in Luckington, opposite the Old Royal Ship Inn.

How to get there *From Acton Turville, follow the B4040 Malmesbury road in a north-easterly direction for 2 miles into Luckington. In the centre of the village, park on the roadside in the vicinity of the green, opposite the Old Royal Ship Inn.*

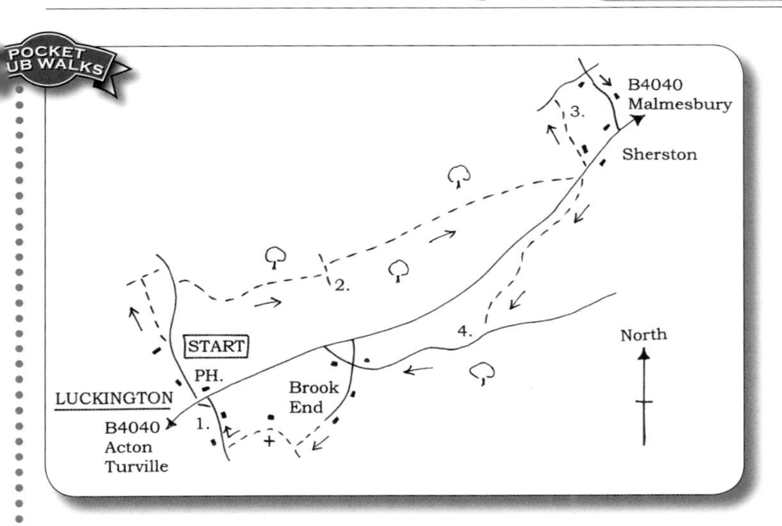

1 Cross the B4040 at the far end of the green opposite a Methodist chapel, and follow the lane signposted to **Sopworth** – appropriately waymarked **Sopworth Road**. In 250 yards, just past a small estate on the left called **Northend**, climb some steps on the left to a gate and open field. Turn right, walking along a short section of enclosed path, before heading across to a stile in the middle of the opposite field boundary. Beyond this stile, head directly across a second field to a gap in the hedgerow opposite, before following the right edge of the next field to a stile in the corner and a farm drive. Turn right and follow this drive along to **Sopworth Road**. Turn right and, in 40 yards, left along a byway. Follow this track for ¾ mile to a junction.

2 Turn left and, in 50 yards, cross a wooden barrier on the right. Walk directly ahead across an open field to a gate in the opposite field boundary, before following the right edge of the next field to a gate in its far right corner. Beyond this gate, follow the right edge of the following field and, where the boundary wall on the right ends, bear half right down to a gateway in the bottom right

A footbridge over the River Avon.

corner of the field and join the B4040. Turn left and, in 150 yards, partway up **Brook Hill**, turn left along an access drive running alongside some stone cottages. Just past the last property – **Silk Mill Cottage** – cross a stile and follow the hillside path ahead above the **River Avon**. Keep on this path as it bears right up to the top boundary wall, before continuing across the hilltop to a stile and lane.

3 Turn right and follow the lane to a crossroads in 200 yards. Turn right into **Court Street** and walk down to its junction with the **High Street** in **Sherston**, opposite the **Rattlebone Inn**. Turn right, walk the length of the **High Street** and continue down to

the bottom of **Brook Hill**. Cross the **River Avon** and immediately cross a stile on the left. Bear right and follow a tributary of the **Avon** across a meadow to a footbridge. Beyond this footbridge, bear right to a stile and continue following the riverside path through scrubland to a hand gate. Cross the hillside field ahead, before turning left to follow the end field boundary uphill to a stile in its top corner. Beyond this stile, bear half left in the next field to a stile and lane.

4 Turn right and follow this lane for ½ mile to the ford in **Brook End**. Follow the raised footbridge alongside the ford to a minor crossroads and turn left to follow a cul-de-sac that runs alongside a number of cottages. Where the lane ends, continue along a raised causeway above the river, before following a grassy path for 150 yards to a junction. Turn right and, in 50 yards, pass through a gate on the left to enter the churchyard alongside **Luckington church**. Follow the path around to the right of the church to a gate in the churchyard wall, and continue along a tarmac path that crosses a field to reach a gate and lane. Turn right and follow this lane back up to the green in the centre of **Luckington**.

Place of interest nearby

Westonbirt Arboretum, just a few miles north of Luckington, is a wonderful world of trees. There are 18,000 of them from all over the world, planted from 1829 to the present day, producing 600 acres of beautiful, landscaped Cotswold countryside. The display of autumn tints is a particularly marvellous sight. For more information ☎ 01666 880220 or visit the website: http://www.forestry.gov.uk/westonbirt.

5 Biddestone

The White Horse

Imagine a typical expatriate sitting on some faraway beach and dreaming of 'Olde England'. There would be a village green with a duckpond, surrounded by stone cottages, and an ancient church somewhere in the background. The other ingredient would, of course, be a traditional hostelry serving real ales and a fine ploughman's lunch. Biddestone would fit the bill perfectly! Here we have what one guidebook called a 'veritable paddling of ducks', whilst the green itself has been described as perhaps 'the most photogenic in the county'. Across the fields, deep in the By Brook valley, lies Slaughterford, a diminutive hamlet with an isolated church, located literally in the middle of a field. It is difficult to think of anywhere that is further from

Distance 4 miles

OS Explorer 156 Chippenham and Bradford on Avon. GR 863735.

An undulating landscape, with one or two climbs in and around the By Brook valley.

Starting point The village green in Biddestone

How to get there *Leave the A4 on the eastern fringes of Corsham by the Cross Keys Inn, and follow the unclassified lane signed to Biddestone. The White Horse and the village green are in the centre of the village.*

the proverbial madding crowd. The By Brook itself, arguably the most attractive of the Avon's tributaries, rises above Castle Combe before joining the Bristol Avon at Bathford. Its clear waters are home to any number of trout, whilst the hanging woodland in the valley provides shelter for hawks and buzzards, owls and kestrels.

THE PUB

The **White Horse** is a charming whitewashed hostelry, dating from the 16th century, with picnic tables overlooking the village green and duck pond in this most English of villages. A wide choice of sensibly priced food is on offer, ranging from filled rolls to hearty pub food. To accompany your meal, why not try a glass of the well-kept Butcombe or Wadworth 6X, fine West Country beers from local brewers.

Open all day on Friday, Saturday, and Sunday; 11.30 am to 2.30 pm and 5 pm to 11 pm during the rest of the week.
☎ *01249 713305*

1 Walk past the duck pond in **Biddestone** and, where the main road bears right, keep ahead into **Church Road**. Having passed the church, turn right into **Challows Lane** and, just past the first rank of cottages on the right, cross a stone slab stile on the right. Follow the right edges of the next two fields to a gap in the hedge in the corner of the second field, before joining a lane. Turn left and follow this lane for ¼ mile to a right-hand bend and a pair of footpaths on the left.

2 Ignoring the path on the immediate left, enter the field ahead. Cross the middle of this field to a stile opposite – just to the right of a telegraph pole – before following a line of electricity wires across the next field to a gate and stile opposite. Follow the right edge of the following field down to a gate and the lane leading into **Slaughterford**. Turn left and follow this lane downhill for ½ mile to a minor road junction immediately past **Manor Farm**. At this point, cross a stile in the hedge on the left and cross the field ahead, passing to the left of **Slaughterford church**. Pass through a hand gate on the far side of the field and drop down to the lane in the centre of the hamlet.

3 Turn right and follow the lane for 150 yards to a bend by a telephone box. Turn left and follow a track alongside a property that leads to a gate and open field. Cross this field – passing to

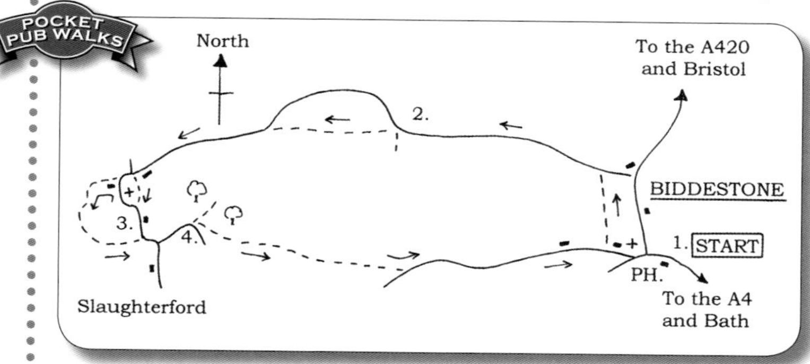

The By Brook.

the left of a pylon – to a telegraph pole in the dip on the far side of the field. Pass through a gap in the hedge and enter a riverside meadow. Walk across to the **By Brook**, and follow the river downstream – to the left – to a sluice and footbridge. Cross the river, turn left and continue following the **By Brook** downstream. On the far side of the field, cross a pair of footbridges before following a wooded path to a gate and lane at the southern end of **Slaughterford**. Follow the lane ahead – the river on the right – to a junction, before following the road ahead for 100 yards to a right-hand bend.

4 On this bend, follow the bridleway directly ahead and – almost immediately – turn right to follow a stepped path up through a wooded bank to a stile. Beyond this stile, continue into a hillside field and walk directly ahead uphill to a belt of trees. Pass through this tree cover and, in the next field, turn right to a stile in the top corner of the field. Cross the middle of the next field to a stile in the opposite field boundary – almost in the right corner of the field. Follow the right edge of the following field for 40 yards and, where the hedge on the right ends, continue across the field, bearing slightly right, to a stile in the right-hand field boundary almost in the corner of the field. Join a lane, turn left and continue for ½ mile back to its junction with **Church Road** in **Biddestone**. Turn left to return to the green.

Biddestone's delightful village pump.

Places of interest nearby

The old market town of **Corsham** lies just a couple miles to the south of Biddestone. Thanks to the prosperity that originated from the medieval wool trade, the town's attractive High Street is lined with many handsome buildings. The town also boasts a stately home, **Corsham Court**. Standing on a former Saxon royal manor, it developed from an Elizabethan manor house of 1582. The quiet street leading to the Court is the site of a folly. Built in 1800, this artificial ruin hid Ethelred House from the west wing of Corsham Court, then Corsham House. For more information about the town, telephone the tourist information centre on ☎ 01249 714660.

6 Box Hill

The Quarryman's Arms

Much of the golden limestone that was used as the building blocks of Georgian Bath came from the extensive network of stone mines that burrowed their way beneath Box Hill, just a few miles east of the city. Today, little remains of this once great industry. There is a monument – in stone, of course – on the hillside, as well as a few overgrown quarry workings on the hilltop and a number of holes in the hillside that give cavers access to the former underground workings. Also this once important industry is commemorated in the name of a local pub, the Quarryman's Arms. Below Box Hill lies the By Brook valley. With its source above Castle Combe, this tributary of the Bristol Avon is a delightful little river, whose clear waters are treasured by trout fishermen, and whose banks are home to kingfisher and heron, coot and moorhen. Hillside and riverside paths, open views, and the chance to see the famous Box Railway tunnel ensure that this fine excursion has an element of interest at every turn.

Distance - 4 miles

OS Explorer 156 Chippenham and Bradford-on-Avon. GR 834693.

Steep hillsides and a valley bottom deep in the southern Cotswolds

Starting point Box Hill Common, near the Quarryman's Arms

How to get there *Box lies on the A4 between Bath and Chippenham. On the eastern side of the village, opposite the Box surgery, turn into Bargates. Follow this estate road up to its junction with Box Hill, turn left and drive uphill to a junction by a small green. Turn left, and continue to Box Hill Common. Park sensibly on the roadside in the vicinity of this common. The Quarryman's Arms lies just a minute or two along the lane.*

THE PUB

Getting to the **Quarryman's Arms** is itself an exciting excursion, but when you arrive you will find a shrine to the former stone mining industry. Old prints and maps adorn the walls, along with former mining implements, creating a haven for the industrial archaeologist. Find yourself a garden table on a summer's day, and you will enjoy a fine view across the By Brook valley towards Colerne. The ever-changing menu is quite superb, with everything from soup and sandwiches to homemade faggots and all-day breakfast, as well as seriously good restaurant-style meals in the evening. The beers include Moles, Butcombe, and Wadworth brews.

Opening hours are 11 am to 11 pm; Sunday, noon to 10.30 pm.
☎ 01225 743569.

1 Walk along the lane and, just beyond the common, you will pass the **Quarryman's Arms** on the left. Continue to a junction, and keep left down **Barnett's Hill** to a crossroads. Follow the lane opposite, **Hedgesparrow Lane**, down to the A4. Cross with care and follow the unclassified lane opposite downhill for 200 yards to a property called **Mills Platt**, turning right immediately after it onto a bridleway. Follow this for ½ mile across the hillside to a lane just past a property on the right. Turn left, and, at a junction in 200 yards, keep left along a cul-de-sac. In 350 yards, just past a pair of properties on the left, turn left and follow a track that winds its way steeply downhill into the **By Brook** valley.

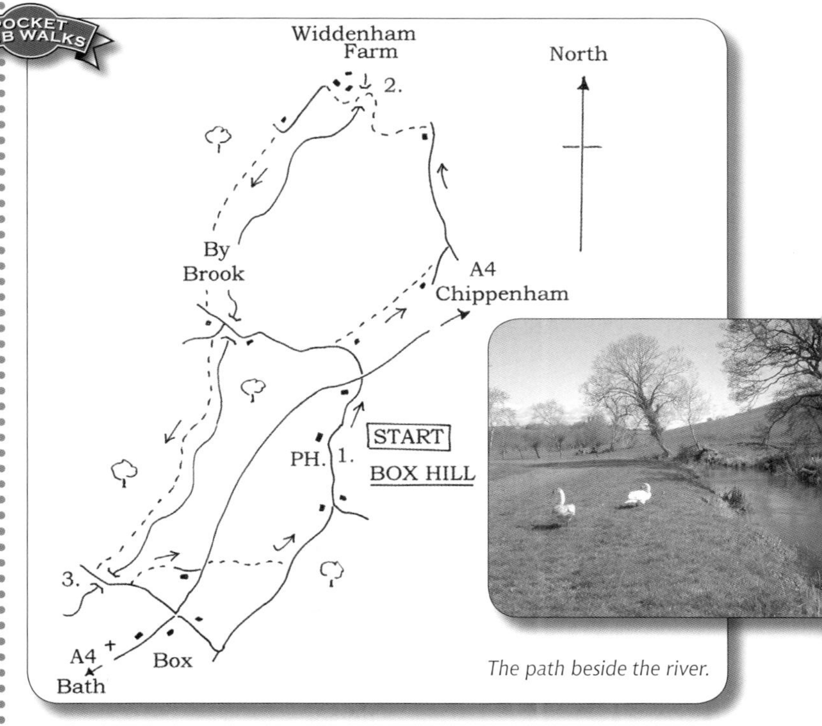

The path beside the river.

2 Cross the **By Brook** and, in ¼ mile, follow a lane to the right skirting the farmhouse to climb out of the valley. In 35 yards, keep on this lane as it bears left and runs along the hillside to reach some farm buildings in 200 yards. On the right-hand bend beyond the farm, pass through a gate ahead and follow a riverside path beside the **By Brook** for ½ mile, crossing two large fields. On the far side of the second field, pass through a gate to join the lane by **Saltbox Farm**. Turn left and, at a junction in 100 yards, turn right. In 100 yards, cross a stile on the left and follow the left edge of the field ahead to a stile. Beyond the stile, bear right and rejoin the **By Brook**. Follow the river for ½ mile across two fields to a stile on the far side of the second field. Immediately past this stile, turn right and follow an enclosed path alongside the river to a footbridge. Cross the bridge, and continue along the path to reach **Mill Lane** in **Box**.

3 Turn left and, in 100 yards, just before a railway bridge, turn left along a narrow enclosed footpath. Follow the path for 200 yards to a road called **The Wharf**, and continue up to the A4. Opposite and slightly to the right is a viewpoint for the **Box railway tunnel**. For the main walk, turn left, and in 75 yards cross a stile opposite to enter a hillside field alongside **Lacy Wood**, the Box Millennium Wood. Follow the fence on the right to the top end of the wood, bear right through an area of scrub at the top of the climb, and cross a stile into the adjoining field. Turn left and climb to the top of the field ahead, where, 50 yards to the right of the corner of the field, a stile gives access to **Box Hill**. Turn left, climb to a hilltop junction and keep left to return to the start.

Places of interest nearby

The Heritage Centre in nearby Corsham features displays relating to **Box Tunnel** and the local stone mines. ☎ 01249 714660 for further information.

7 Doynton

The Cross House

It is fascinating to see how the underlying geology shapes the human landscape. Around Bath, limestone is the dominant bedrock, providing the building blocks for those handsome Georgian terraces that so typify the city. Just a few miles away on the former Bristol coalfield, it is the somewhat dour millstone grit. This makes for rather more characterful and rugged settlements such as Doynton, the starting point for this walk. Beyond Doynton, it is hills all the way, a walk of climbs and descents with some spectacular outlooks to enjoy. Initially there is the climb onto Tog Hill, with views across Bristol towards Wales, the Mendip Hills and north Somerset. This is followed by a descent into the Swainswick valley, a landscape of sweeping hillsides and grand vistas, before a climb onto the Cotswold plateau at the aptly-named Cold Ashton. This marks the end of the uphill sections, and it is now downhill all the way back into Doynton, with an exceptional outlook across the Severn Vale. Such were the hills along the way that I found myself performing a quick calculation: the various uphill sections combine to over 1,000 ft of climbing, quite some feat – no pun intended! – for a walk on the doorstep of Bath and Bristol.

The **Cross House**, dating from the 18th century, has earned regular plaudits on account of its friendly and helpful landlord and staff. This hospitality extends to both the regulars – whether cricket or darts teams – and visitors from outside the

Distance 6 miles

OS Explorer 155 Bristol and Bath. GR 719740.

Steep hillsides in and around the Cotswold escarpment

Starting point The Cross House at Doynton

How to get there *The A420 runs from Bristol to Chippenham. At Wick, just outside Bristol and just before Tog Hill, follow the unclassified road northwards into Doynton and park in the centre of the village in the vicinity of the Cross House.*

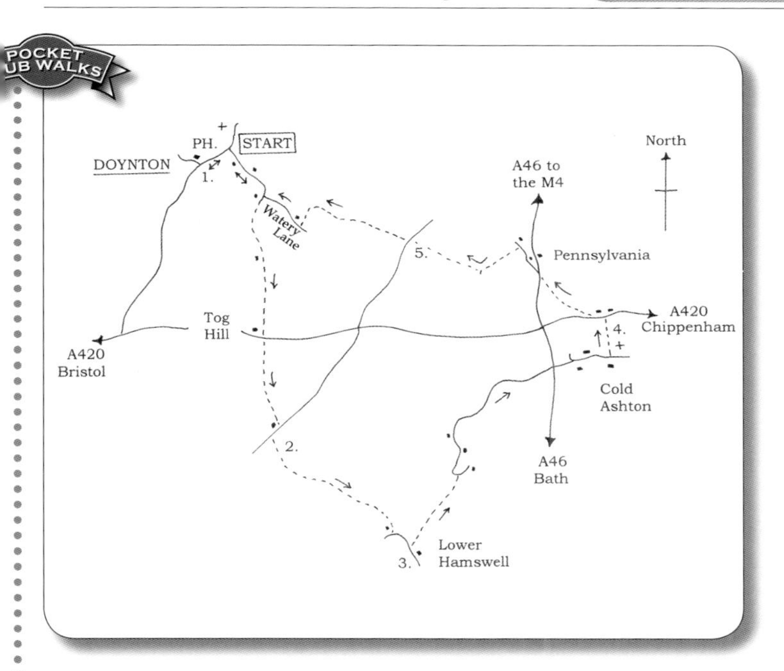

village. Customers can expect an excellent choice of food ranging from sandwiches and soup to pork faggots and steak and kidney pie, as well as a selection of real ales that could include London Pride, Old Speckled Hen and Draught Bass. With beams, stripped stone, and a log fire, the Cross House is everything that could be expected of a traditional village hostelry.

Opening hours are 11.30 am to 3 pm and 6 pm to 11 pm; Sunday, noon to 4 pm and 7 pm to 10.30 pm
☎ *0117 937 2261*

1 Follow the main road in **Doynton**, in the direction of **Dyrham**; in 100 yards, turn right into **Toghill Lane**. In 300 yards, at a junction where **Watery Lane** goes off on the left, keep walking ahead along an unclassified lane for 600 yards to a property called **Babwell Farm**; then continue for ½ mile along a track that climbs up to the A420 on **Tog Hill**. Cross the main road with care and follow the footpath opposite for 200 yards uphill to a gate. Continue ahead across the bottom end of a paddock to a gateway opposite; then follow the path across the right edge of a hillside field, with fine views to the right towards Bristol. In the far corner of this field, follow a track out to a busy rat-run from Bath to the M4 motorway.

2 Follow the road to the right for 100 yards, before taking the driveway on the left-hand side of the road leading to **Hamswell House**. In 20 yards, cross a stile on the right and walk ahead across the middle of a small field to a stile in the opposite hedgerow. Beyond the stile, bear half left towards the left-hand field boundary, which is out of sight over the crest of the hill. When the hedgerow comes into view, make for a stile 100 yards below the corner of the field. Follow the left edge of the next field downhill to the bottom corner of the field, pass through a gateway on the right by a property, and follow the drive to its junction with a lane; go left here, down towards **Lilliput Farm**.

3 Just before the farm, turn left to a stile and follow the **Cotswold Way** across a field to a gateway opposite. Continue walking in the same direction to a gateway in the far left corner of the next field, with a pond on the right, and then cross to a hand gate in the far left corner of the third field. Continue through a small wooded area to a lane, and follow this byway to the left, uphill. Beyond **Hill Farm**, continue along the lane for ½ mile to its junction with the A46. Follow the lane opposite to a junction in **Cold Ashton**, before taking the lane to the right through the village. In 500 yards, follow a track on the left up to the church, pass to the left of the church, and continue along what is still the **Cotswold Way** to a gate; walk on alongside a driveway down to the A420.

A hilltop view.

4 Turn left past the **White Hart** and some cottages, before passing through a gateway on the right into a field. Walk diagonally across the middle of the field to a stile in the far corner. In the next field, head across the far left corner to the A46 in **Pennsylvania**, which should be crossed with extreme care. Follow the lane opposite that passes to the left of a pair of cottages. In 200 yards, just before the next group of cottages, pass through a gap in the wall on the left and follow a path directly ahead alongside a farm compound. Where the fence on the left ends, keep ahead across the field to some conifers opposite; turn right past the trees to walk down to a gate in the corner of the field leading to **Gorse Lane**.

5 Cross a stile opposite and walk ahead across a hilltop field to a stile in the bottom boundary, 450 yards distant and some 75 yards along from the far right corner of the field. Drop downhill to a stile in the bottom corner of the next field and, beyond this stile, cross another on the left into the adjoining field. Follow the right edges of the following three fields to a stile on the right, 200 yards across the third field. Beyond this stile, follow the right edge of the next field down to a gateway opposite and a green lane. Follow this to the left for 250 yards to its junction with **Watery Lane**, turn right and follow this quiet back road for 300 yards to its junction with **Toghill Lane**. Turn right, and retrace your steps down the main road in **Doynton**; then turn left, back to the **Cross House.**

Place of interest nearby

Dyrham Park, a National Trust property with a spectacular late-17th-century mansion, garden, and deer park lies just a few miles from Doynton, on the A46 between Bath and the M4 motorway. Film buffs will recognise Dyrham as the setting for *The Remains of the Day* (1993). ☎ 0117 937 2501 for more information or visit the National Trust's website.

8 Kelston

The Old Crown

The Cotswolds Area of Outstanding Natural Beauty ends in the Bath and Bradford-on-Avon area, a boundary marked by a change in the underlying bedrock. Along the AONB's southern boundary to the north-west of Bath lie villages such as North Stoke and Upton Cheyney, below which quite substantial hillsides tumble down towards the settlements of Kelston and Kelston Mill and the banks of the River Avon. This attractive, vulnerable countryside lying between Bath and Bristol provides the walker with a fine panoramic view across these two historic

Distance 6 miles

OS Explorer 155 Bristol and Bath. GR 701672.

A gradual climb onto Kelston Round Hill followed by easy walking

Starting point The cul-de-sac leading to Kelston church, just a short walk from the Old Crown at Kelston

How to get there *The A431 runs north of the River Avon between Bristol and Bath, passing through Kelston. At the eastern end of the village, just past the Old Crown, turn into the cul-de-sac that heads south to the church. Park on the roadside.*

and greatly contrasting cities. Further afield, the eye can glimpse Dundry Hill and the Mendips to the south of Bristol, as well as the more distant Welsh Mountains. The grandeur of this outlook contrasts with the more intimate and relaxing stroll along the path beside the Avon, on a walk of great variety, with interest at every turn.

THE PUB

The **Old Crown**, built from local stone, dates from the 17th century. It presents a bright frontage to passing traffic, with its hanging baskets and barrels of flowers. This traditional hostelry, with its low ceilings and bunches of hops, flagstone floors, and open fires, has quite rightly earned the praise of local reviewers. The reasonably-priced food includes some excellent salads, and, as part of the Butcombe estate, a pint of their Gold or Blonde comes highly recommended. To quote the website: 'No machines or music, just good beer, good food, good wine, and good company. Not just a pub... more a way of life!' A perfect description.

Opening hours are 11.30 am to 2.30 pm and 5 pm to 11 pm; Saturday, 11 am to 11 pm; Sunday, noon to 10.30 pm
☎ *01225 423032*

1 Walk back to the main road, turn right and follow the road in the direction of **Bath**. In 200 yards, just past the last property on the left in **Kelston**, a track goes off to a gateway on the left. Ignoring this track, continue for 20 yards to a second track on the left, marked with a footpath sign, and follow it up to a gate and an open field. Follow the grassy track ahead as it climbs gently uphill across four fields. At the far side of the fourth field, cross a stile and cross the field ahead to a stile immediately to the left of **Dean Hill House**. Follow the right edge of the next field to a stile in its far right corner; then follow the track ahead for 150 yards

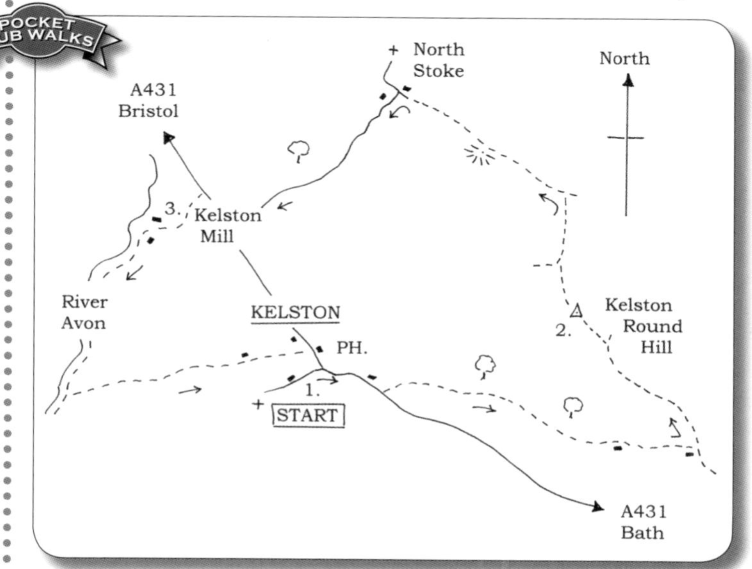

Above the Avon valley.

to its junction with another track alongside **Pendean Farm**. Turn left – the track is the **Cotswold Way** – and continue for just over ½ mile to a point where the track bears right, just below **Kelston Round Hill**. At this point, pass through a hand gate on the left and climb to the hilltop.

2 Pass to the left of the clump of trees on the hilltop to the trig point; continue to a stile and follow the trees on the hilltop around to the right to reach a seat. At this point, bear left and drop downhill to a stile in the bottom corner of the field before joining a track. Turn right and follow the track for 400 yards to a gate and a junction with another track. Turn left, and follow this track for ¾ mile to a back lane in **North Stoke**. Continue to a junction in the village, turn left, and drop downhill for ½ mile to reach the A431. (Alternatively, detour to the right in **North Stoke** if you wish to explore the village and its church.) Turn right and, in 100 yards, cross a stile in the hedge on the left. Walk directly ahead across a riverside meadow to reach a footbridge and stile on the far side of the field. In the next field, follow the right-hand field boundary round to some properties. On the far side of the field, beyond a hand gate, follow a path between two houses to a lane. Cross the lane, and walk towards the cottages opposite. Follow the path directly in front of these houses to a stile, bear right, and follow a path down to a stile by the **River Avon**.

3 Follow the riverside path upstream for ½ mile, pass underneath an old railway bridge, and continue in the next field. In 200 yards, turn left away from the river, and head across to a railway bridge; pass under the former railway. Follow the track ahead gently uphill to a gate and then continue along the right edge of the next field to a gate and a small compound. Beyond the compound, follow a track ahead towards some farm buildings. Cross a stile in the fence to the right of the buildings, before following the left edge of the field ahead to a stile and a track. Turn left to a hand gate, cross a farm track to a stile opposite and continue along an enclosed path up to the A431. Turn right here to reach the **Old Crown**, and the next right is the cul-de-sac where the walk started.

Place of interest nearby

Bitton, just a mile or two west of Kelston, is the home of the **Avon Valley Railway**. This is Bristol and Bath's closest preserved railway, and offers steam and diesel-hauled trips on a three-mile section of the former Midland Railway line between Mangotsfield and Bath Green Park. Contact the railway on ☎ 0117 932 5538 for further information or visit the website on http://www.avonvalleyrailway.co.uk.

9 Norton St Philip

The George Inn

Maxwell Fraser's *Companion into Somerset* describes a country lane leading to Norton St Philip. He writes of a settlement that is 'too lovely to be overlooked or neglected'. What caught Fraser's eye was the enchanting black and white inn, reputed to be the oldest in England, a fine old church, and much natural and man-made beauty. Behind that inn, named the George, lies a large open green known as the Mead, that runs down to the parish church. It is the tower that dominates the scene – 70 feet of lovingly crafted stone that allegedly brought Samuel Pepys to this corner of Somerset. Round about is a landscape of hillsides and valleys, with diminutive streams that eventually flow into the Bristol Avon. This is neither the Mendip Hills nor the Cotswolds, but rather countryside that blends characteristics of the two, with stone cottages and farmsteads, narrow and infrequently used country lanes, and grand vistas. All the better for being pleasant rather than spectacular, this little-visited part of the area is perfect for restoring a contented mien.

THE PUB

Doing justice to the **George Inn** in a single paragraph is impossible; so a few facts! A pub for 600 years, this ancient hostelry was originally built to house the merchants buying wool and cloth from nearby Hinton Priory. Heavy beams and oak panelling abound, together with grand stone fireplaces and a sense of history that is confirmed by the recorded presence here of the Duke of Monmouth, prior to the Battle of Sedgemoor. Both light meals and a restaurant-style menu are available, with options ranging from cold meat or cheese platter to steak, mushroom and ale pie, and local trout with roasted almonds. A glass of Wadworth 6X or IPA makes the perfect accompaniment.

Opening hours are: 10.30 am to 2.30 pm and 5.30 pm to 11 pm; Saturday, 10.30 am to 11 pm; Sunday, noon to 3 pm and 7 pm to 10.30 pm.

☎ *01373 834224; website: www.thegeorgeinn-nsp.co.uk*

Distance 4½ miles

OS Explorer 142 Shepton Mallet and Mendip Hills East. GR 772557.

Hillsides and valleys to the west of Norton St Philip

Starting point Vicarage Lane in Norton St Philip, separated from the George Inn by the Mead

How to get there *Norton St Philip lies on the B3110 Woolverton road, 5 miles south of Bath. In the centre of the village, alongside the George Inn, turn right onto the A366 road for Radstock. In 250 yards, turn left into Vicarage Lane and park alongside the village church.*

1 Return to the A366, turn left along **Church Street**, and take the first right into **Ringwell Lane**. Follow **Ringwell Lane** for 250 yards to a crossroads. Turn left into **Wellow Lane** and follow this quiet road for just over 1 mile to a ford and footbridge on the left. Cross the **Norton Brook** at this point, and follow the byway ahead for 1 mile to **Upper Baggridge Farm**, ignoring a right turn to **Lower Baggridge Farm** along the way. Walk through the farmyard to reach a lane and follow it for ½ mile. Immediately before an area of woodland on the left called **Baggridge Belt**, turn left through a hand gate.

2 Follow the right edges of the next two fields and, on reaching the bottom corner of the second field, turn left to follow its lower boundary. In 150 yards, follow the bridleway as it bears right through a gateway into the adjoining field. Follow the left edge of the field ahead to its lower left-hand corner, join a track, and continue for 350 yards up to a farming hamlet called **Hassage**. Where the drive bears right up to some farm buildings, keep ahead along an unmetalled track and continue for 400 yards until an old barn appears on the right, ignoring a left turn along the way. Beyond the old barn, follow the track into a field and continue ahead to a point where the hedge on the left ends.

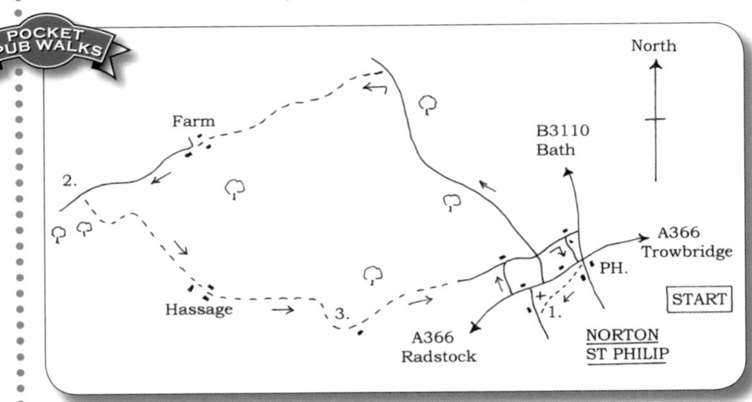

Bear right here and head downhill towards **Mount Pleasant Farm**. At the bottom of the field, pass through a gate and follow the track down the left edge of the next field to a gate and footbridge crossing a stream.

A quiet byway on the walk.

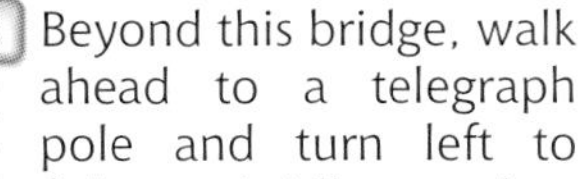

3 Beyond this bridge, walk ahead to a telegraph pole and turn left to follow a bridleway along the edge of a field, the boundary on the left-hand side. In 200 yards, beyond a gateway, follow an enclosed track for 600 yards back to **Ringwell Lane** in **Norton**. Turn left, and follow this lane to a crossroads in 100 yards. Follow the road opposite, **Chevers Lane**, and continue uphill for 150 yards before turning right into **North Street**. Follow this back road to the A366, and turn left to the **George Inn**. Just before the inn, pass through a hand gate and follow an alley alongside the inn to the local recreation ground, which you cross to a gate in the churchyard wall opposite. Walk through the churchyard and return to **Vicarage Lane**.

Place of interest nearby

Just south of Norton St Philip, signed from the A36 roundabout at Beckington, is the **Whiterow Farm Shop**, an unusual attraction, but well worth the visit if you are attracted by local produce. Here we find Somerset ciders and cheeses, free range eggs, and local beef, lamb, chicken, and duck. With a gift shop and tearoom, this makes an interesting diversion.

☎ 01373 830798 for more information.

10 Wellow

The Fox & Badger

Driving west from Hinton Charterhouse, the motorist suddenly encounters a rather fine outlook towards Wellow, with its grand houses and stone cottages clinging to a south-facing hillside above the Wellow Brook, the whole overseen by the massive tower of St Julian's church. All around lies an impressive natural landscape, where the outlying hills of the Cotswolds and the Mendips meet and merge to form a green undulating tapestry of low hills, valleys and narrow winding lanes, bordered by hedgerows. To the north of Wellow, in a neighbouring valley, lies the equally charming village of Combe Hay, set against a backdrop of wooded hillside. Deep in the woodland lie the decaying remains of the Combe Hay locks on the Somerset Coal Canal, 22 locks that replaced unsuccessful attempts to descend the hillside using initially a caisson lock and latterly an inclined plane.

THE PUB

The **Fox & Badger**, originally known as the New Inn, dates from way back in the 16th century. Flagstones and log fires add to a most traditional atmosphere in this unspoiled and cosy pub. There is a menu to suit all tastes, with selections ranging from sandwiches and baguettes to steaks, fish and poultry dishes, whilst the good selection of real ales might include Butcombe Bitter and Badgers Best. The landlord being a master cheesemaker, the ploughman's comes particularly recommended.

Opening hours are Monday to Thursday 11.30 am to 3.30 pm and 6 pm to 11 pm; Friday and Saturday, 11.30 am to 11 pm; Sunday, noon to 10.30 pm
☎ *01225 832293; website: www.foxandbadger.co.uk*

Distance 5 miles

OS Explorers 142 Shepton Mallet and Mendip Hills East and 155 Bath and Bristol. GR 739583.

Steep hillsides, a valley bottom and some potentially damp paths

Starting point The Fox & Badger in Wellow

How to get there *Leave the B3110 road at Hinton Charterhouse, 5 miles south of Bath, and follow the unclassified road signed to Wellow. On reaching the centre of the village, park in the Square outside the Fox & Badger.*

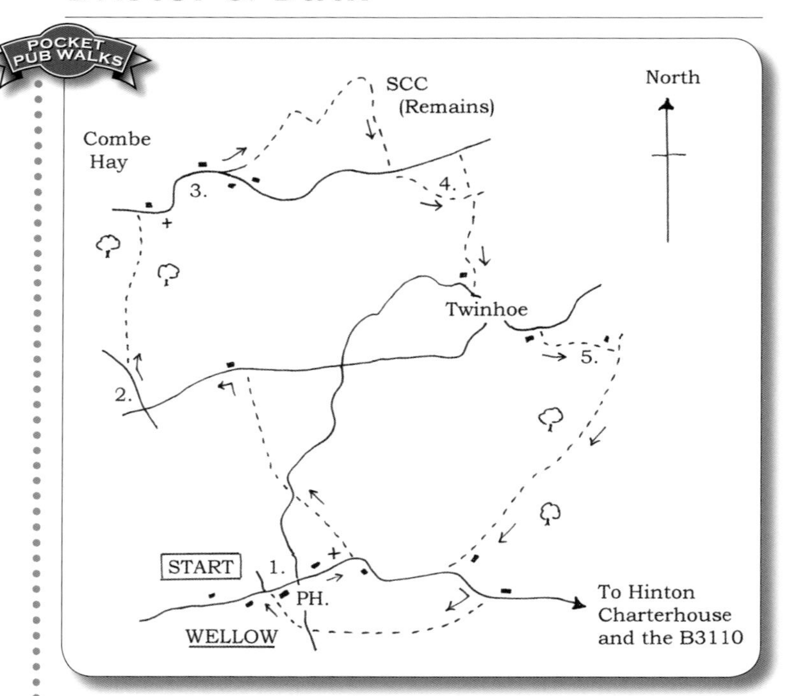

1 With your back to the pub, turn right along the main street in **Wellow** and walk as far as **St Julian's church**. Immediately past the church, turn left along an access lane and walk to a gate and stile. Beyond the stile, follow an enclosed path along the left edge of a paddock to another stile. In the next field, walk uphill to a stile in the far boundary, 20 yards to the left of a gate. Cross a lane to a stile opposite and follow the right edge of the field ahead up to a stile and a large arable field. In the following field, head for a telegraph pole, bear half left to a 'corner' formed by the boundaries of the field ahead, and follow the line of the field boundary uphill to a stile in the top boundary, 100 yards to the right of some barns on the skyline. At the lane, turn left and walk along the hilltop for 600 yards to a crossroads.

2 Turn right – waymarked to **Bath** and **Combe Hay** – and follow the road for 250 yards to a footpath on the right, where the road begins to drop downhill through some woodland. Follow the footpath into a hillside field above **Combe Hay**, turn left,

The ford at Wellow.

and drop downhill to a marker post above a belt of trees. Go downhill through the trees to a hand gate, before crossing the following field to a hand gate opposite. Beyond the gate and a belt of trees, cross a stile and footbridge into the next field, which you cross, bearing slightly left, to a hand gate opposite. Then climb a grassy bank to some trees, a hand gate, and the road in **Combe Hay**. Turn right, and follow the road as it winds its way through Combe Hay, bearing left by the church and right by a property called **Meribah**, to reach the **Wheatsheaf Inn**.

Part of the Somerset Coal Canal.

3 Continue past the **Wheatsheaf** for 200 yards, before forking left along a lane that leads to **Rowley Farm**. Continue to a property called **East Rowley**, where the lane becomes a track. Follow this track for 200 yards to a gate. Cross the stile on the right, and drop down the right edge of a field to enter **Engine Wood** via a track in the bottom corner of the field. Some 15 yards along this track, cross a stile on the left and follow a path alongside an early cut of the Somerset Coal Canal (SCC). Follow this path as it drops downhill through woodland to reach part of the canal known as the **Bullnose**. Cross a footbridge over a stream; then, in 20 yards, follow the path to the right that borders the locks on the SCC. Follow this path down to a gate, an overbridge, and a lane. Cross the lane to a hand gate opposite and follow an enclosed path for 300 yards to a gate and junction.

4 Turn right and follow a track across the **Cam Brook** and uphill through trees, emerging onto an open track in 350 yards. Follow this track uphill to the lane in **Twinhoe**. Turn left and follow the

hilltop road for 350 yards, ignoring one right turn but then turning right into the drive leading to **Middle Twinhoe Barns**. Just before the properties, bear left along a grassy path to a gate. Cross to a hand gate in the far left corner of the next field, before bearing half-left in the next field to an old gateway in its far left corner. In the next corner, follow a sunken path on the right that runs just below the level of the field. Keep on this path for 250 yards until it joins a track coming down from **Lower Twinhoe Farm**.

5 Turn right and follow the track downhill, under a railway bridge, and on towards the valley bottom. Beyond a gate, turn right and follow an enclosed path across the top of a meadow and then for 600 yards until it enters an open field. Keeping to the level, follow the path across the field to a fence line on the far side. Follow the path ahead to reach the road leading to **Wellow**. Turn left and follow the road downhill into the valley bottom. Just before a property, cross a stile on the right and follow a riverside path across six fields, bordering the **Wellow Brook**. Cross a gate on the far side of the sixth field, and cross the lane ahead, walking towards a packhorse bridge. Turn right by the bridge and follow a gravelled path uphill back into Wellow. At the top of the climb, cross the old **Somerset & Devon Railway** and follow the back lane ahead to the **Fox & Badger**.

Place of interest nearby

The **Radstock Museum** offers an insight into the way of life of this former coal-mining town in the heart of the North Somerset coalfield. With awards that range from the Civic Trust Award to the Green Tourism Award, and comments from visitors such as 'a fascinating trip down memory lane', a trip to this excellent museum is highly recommended. ☎ 01761 437722 or visit www.radstockmuseum.co.uk for more information.

11 Stanton Drew

The Druids Arms

In 1967, Adge Cutler and the Wurzels penned a song entitled 'When the Common Market Comes to Stanton Drew', placing this North Somerset village firmly on the road to immortality. In all fairness, Stanton Drew already had a reputation that stretched far and wide on account of its ancient stone circle. To be more precise, this huge megalithic complex consists of three stone circles, two stone avenues, a cove of stones, and an outlier. On the hilltop above Stanton Drew is another ancient monument in the form of Maes Knoll. This commanding hillfort enjoys an expansive outlook, a literal 360° panorama. To the north lies the whole of the Greater Bristol conurbation, stretching away towards the Cotswold Hills and the Severn Vale, whilst the view to the south extends across the Chew Valley and on towards the Mendip Hills. Be sure to pick a fine clear day for what, with its open hilltops and wide-ranging vistas, must be the best hill walk on the doorstep of the West Country's largest city.

Distance 5 miles

OS Explorer 155 Bristol and Bath. GR 598631.

Steep hillsides so a fairly energetic excursion

Starting point The car park for the Cove Stone, alongside the Druids Arms in Stanton Drew

How to get there *Leave the B3130 road one mile east of Chew Magna, and turn into Stanton Drew village. In ¼ mile, there is a two-level car park just past the Druids Arms. Park on the higher level, alongside the Cove Stone. Alternatively, just before the Druids Arms, the village hall car park is on the right-hand side.*

THE PUB

Located near Stanton Drew's prehistoric stone circle, the **Druids Arms** boasts some standing stones of its own in the beer garden. As well as hosting boules matches and occasional barbecues, this popular village inn serves delicious home-cooked food, including enormous portions of faggots with chips or a spicy chilli, all for very reasonable prices. The local real ales include Wadworth 6X and Smiles Best, as well as locally brewed guest ales on weekly rotation.

Opening hours are 11 am to 2.30 pm and 6 pm to 11 pm.
☎ *01275 332230*

1 Follow the road back through **Stanton Drew** village, cross the **River Chew** and continue to the junction with the B3130 beside the thatched tollhouse. Turn right and, in just 75 yards, turn left along an unmarked side road. Follow this lane for ¾ mile into **Norton Malreward**, ignoring a left turn along the way. Continue

through the village for 350 yards to a junction. Turn left, signed to **Dundry** and **North Wick**, and, in 20 yards, pass through a hand gate on the right into a hillside field. Follow the left edge of the field steeply uphill to a hand gate in the top corner; then bear left to the next hand gate in the left-hand boundary and a hilltop track.

2 Turn right, towards the ramparts of **Maes Knoll**. Continue across the left edge of the hilltop field to a hand gate, which you pass through before turning right and following the edge of the hilltop to another rampart, with superb views all the while across the **Chew Valley**. Follow the edge of the rampart to the right, down to the end of the field. Turn left and continue along the edge of the hilltop to a hand gate, hedgerows blocking the view across Bristol. Go through the gate and follow a path across an open hilltop to a stile and a lane. Turn left and follow the lane for ¾ mile to a gate and signed footpath on the left.

3 Go through the gate and follow the left edge of the field down to a gate in the bottom corner. Go through this gate also, follow

The ancient stones at Stanton Drew.

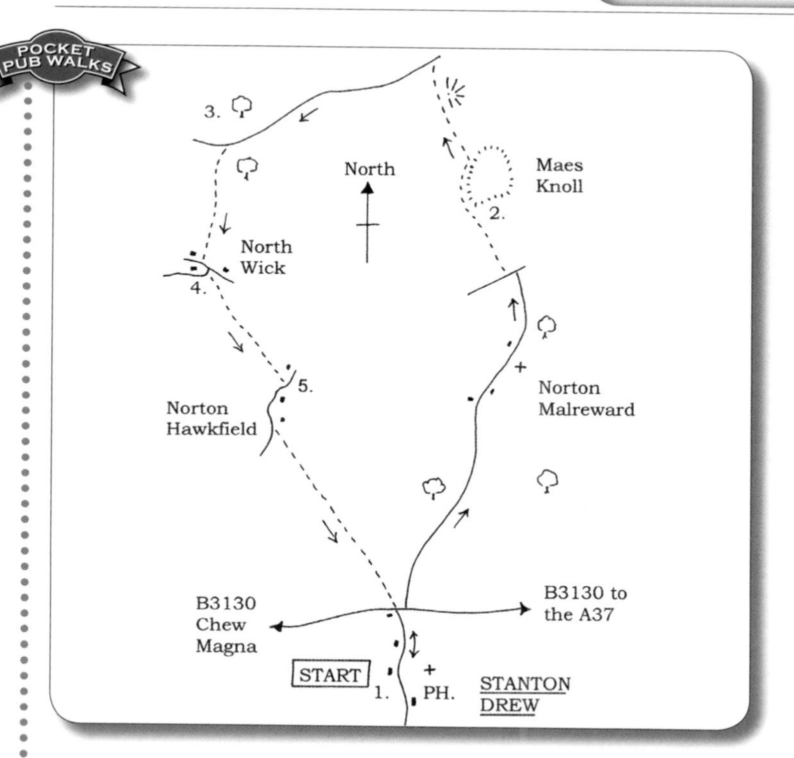

the right edge of the next field to a gate in the corner. Follow the right edge of the next field for 150 yards to a gate on the right, before walking diagonally across the middle of the adjoining field to a stile in the opposite corner. Cross the stile, bear half left, and drop downhill towards some properties in **North Wick**. Keep to the left of an area of scrubland, before crossing a stile at the bottom of the field to join the lane in **North Wick**.

4 Turn left to a junction by **Leat House**, before taking the right turn to **Dundry**. In 20 yards, cross a stile on the left and head across a field to a stile opposite; then follow the left edge of the next field to a footbridge over a stream. Cross the bridge, turn left, and walk along the bottom left edge of the following field to a stile. Continue along the bottom left edge of the next field to a stile, before walking along the left edge of the following field for just 20 yards to a footbridge on the left. Beyond this footbridge, turn right and walk the whole length of the field ahead to another footbridge; then walk through an area of scrubland to a stile. Cross the stile and bear half left, clipping the corner of a field, to a stile leading into the lane in **Norton Hawkfield**.

5 Turn right and, in 300 yards, on a right-hand bend, climb some steps on the left to a hand gate. Cross the field ahead to a visible stile opposite then follow the left edge of the next field to a stile. In the following field, cross to a stile in the far right corner, before dropping downhill to a stile in the bottom right corner of the next field. Good views open up across the Chew Valley. In the adjoining field, follow the right-hand boundary to a stile in the corner, and, in one final field, head across to a hand gate to the right of Stanton Drew garage. Join the B3130 and turn right to a junction by the thatched tollhouse before turning left, back into **Stanton Drew**.

Place of interest nearby

Chew Valley Lake, just to the west of Stanton Drew, was built as a reservoir to supply the city of Bristol in 1956. The reservoir provides a thriving leisure facility for sailors, fishermen, ornithologists and picnickers. A number of hides around the lake allow you to watch some of the 250 species of wildfowl that live on and around the lake. To make the most of Chew Valley Lake, go to the teashop at the northern end of the lake. As well as an enjoyable cream tea or coffee, you will be able to explore a gift shop that sells books, pamphlets, and postcards relating to this delightful stretch of open water. ☎ 01275 333345.

12 East Harptree

The Waldegrave Arms

'No pain no gain' – so this impressive walk on the Mendip Hills begins with a stiff climb out of East Harptree onto a lofty hilltop perch! It's quite some climb, but one that will provide plenty of opportunities to pause for breath and to take in the views. High on the hilltops lies East Harptree Wood, whose main feature of interest is Smitham Chimney. Strange as it may seem, the woodland site was the scene of intense industrial activity back in the 1850s, when lead, silver, and calamine were mined and smelted locally. A steep descent off the hills brings the walk into the secluded and secretive world of Harptree Combe. This narrow limestone gorge contains a variety of habitats that include ash woodland and rough grassland, natural and artificial rock faces, and a small marshy stream. The flora is rich and

Distance 4½ miles

OS Explorer 141 Cheddar Gorge and Mendip Hills West. GR 565560.

Hilly in the Mendips; with the possibility of muddy paths in Harptree Combe

Starting point East Harptree church alongside the Waldegrave Arms.

How to get there *Leave the A368 at West Harptree, midway between Bath and Weston-super-Mare, and follow the B3114 towards East Harptree. In ½ mile, turn right into the village centre and, on reaching a junction by the village store, turn right into Church Lane. Follow this side road to the church, where there are parking spaces directly opposite the Waldegrave Arms.*

varied, and includes herb Paris and small teasel, autumn crocus and 'an increasingly rare plant, listed in the Red Data Book as one of the most vulnerable components of the British flora' – the Natural England website reveals no more!

THE PUB

The **Waldegrave Arms** is an attractive 17th-century inn, in which log fires and cosy dining rooms provide a warm welcome for visitors. For summer days, there is also a large landscaped garden, where customers can rest and linger awhile, perhaps with a bottle of fine wine, for which the hostelry is well known. The midweek lunch specials represent excellent value for money, with such options as asparagus and mushroom omelette or loin of pork, following starters that might include goats' cheese crouton and soup. Fine food, fine drink and a fine walk – what more could one ask for?

Opening hours are noon to 2.30 pm and 6 pm to 11 pm.
☎ 01761 221429; website: www.waldegravearmseastharptree.co.uk

1 Walk down **Church Lane** to the village store and follow **Whitecross Road** ahead for 300 yards to a stile and a footpath on the right, immediately past an orchard. Cross the stile and follow the right edge of three fields to a stile and lane alongside some properties. Turn left for just 15 yards, before turning right and

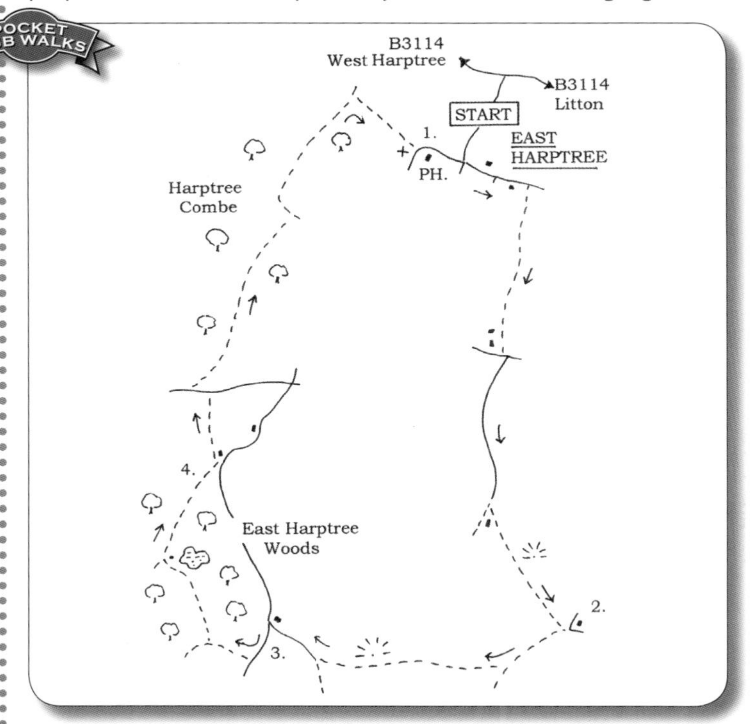

following a side lane for 600 yards to a detached property with a track to the left. Follow the track for 150 yards and, at its end, pass through a hand gate on the right to enter a hillside field. Head uphill to a stile in the top boundary, just past an isolated tree and, in the following field, head across to a stile in the fence opposite, passing to the right of a telegraph pole along the way. Beyond the stile, walk ahead to a stile in the hedgerow opposite; cross the next field, bearing slightly left all the while, to a stile in the opposite field boundary and a track.

Smitham Chimney.

2 Follow the track around to the left to its junction with another track in just 50 yards, immediately before a lane and a property. Turn right and follow this stony track uphill for 300 yards to a gate and a footpath on the right marked with a **Monarch's Way** marker, ignoring a slightly earlier gateway on the right. Follow the right edge of this field to a gateway opposite and, in the next field, head across to a stile in the opposite boundary, almost in the far left-hand corner. Beyond the stile, follow the left edge of the next field to a gate and track, before continuing along a lane for 250 yards to a road junction just above **Nettwood Farm**. Turn left to follow the lane for 150 yards before taking a right turn into the Forestry Commission's **East Harptree Wood** complex.

3 Follow the drive ahead and, where it bears left into a parking area, keep ahead along a gated track. In 400 yards, on a left-hand bend, turn right along a waymarked path to **Smitham Chimney**. Keep on this path as far as a junction alongside the chimney at the western end of a pond. Turn right here and follow the path behind the chimney, continuing downhill to an exit gate from the woodland in 150 yards. Beyond the gate, follow a track for 150 yards, passing a farm complex on the left, before turning left at a gate and stile on the left, just before a house and a lane.

4 Cross a cattle-feeding compound; then walk across an open field to a stile in the middle of the far boundary. In the next field, drop downhill to a stile in the bottom right corner, bear right to a second stile and turn left to drop down the left edge of the adjoining field to a stile and lane. Turn left here and, in 50 yards, pass through a hand gate on the right before walking across the bottom of a field to a gate at the entrance to **Harptree Combe**, 50 yards ahead. Follow the path through the combe for ½ mile until it bears right and drops down to a junction. Keep left at this junction and continue following a stream through the combe for 500 yards to a gate and stile. Turn right and climb a steep bank before walking the length of a narrow field to a stile in the far boundary. Bear half right in the next field to a stile alongside **East Harptree church**. Continue along the path, back to the parking area.

Place of interest nearby

Wells, the smallest city in England, lies just a few miles south of East Harptree. As well as the internationally renowned cathedral, visitors to Wells can enjoy the delights of the moated Bishop's Palace, as well as the various displays in the Wells and Mendip Museum. For more information, contact the local tourist information centre on ☎ 01749 672552.

13 Blagdon

The New Inn

Blagdon nestles on the north-facing slopes of the Mendip Hills, overlooking the Chew Valley and Blagdon Lake, one of the nation's best trout fisheries. Construction of a dam on the River Yeo began in 1891 and the reservoir finally reached top level in 1903. Across the hills from Blagdon lies Burrington Combe, where a cleft in a rock face provided shelter from a storm for Augustus Toplady, the local vicar. This was the inspiration – or so the story goes – for that much loved hymn 'Rock of Ages'. The shelter and shade of Burrington is in complete contrast to the open moorland of Blackdown, where, at 1,068 ft above sea-level, Beacon Batch is the Mendips' literal high point. The views from this lofty hilltop perch are naturally wide-ranging and include, far below, the village of Blagdon and the delights of the New Inn.

THE PUB

The **New Inn** is a handsome cottage-style hostelry dating from the 17th century. The two bar areas offer a warm and traditional welcome to customers, especially if you are lucky enough to be seated close to the logs that crackle away in the inn's inglenook fireplaces. Around the walls are tankards and horse brasses, as well as local prints and the occasional farming artefact, a reminder that we are in the heart of the West Country. Visit the New Inn during the summer and there can be few better views than the one from the garden that takes in Blagdon Lake and the Chew Valley Lake. The menu extends from starters and lunchtime snacks to steak and poultry dishes, a wide selection of seafood and a number of vegetarian options and, as this is a Wadworth house, a pint of 6X is almost obligatory.

Opening hours are Tuesday to Saturday, 11 am to 2.30 pm and 7 pm to 11 pm; Sunday, noon to 3 pm and 7 pm to 10.30 pm. Closed all day Monday.
☎ *01761 462475*

Distance 6½ miles

OS Explorer 141 Cheddar Gorge and Mendip Hills West. GR 504589.

Includes a steep climb onto the Mendips' high point

Starting point Blagdon church, less than a minute's walk from the New Inn

How to get there *Leave the A368 Weston-super-Mare to Bath road on the eastern edge of Blagdon and turn into Church Street. In 250 yards, just before the New Inn, turn left at a small green and park in the cul-de-sac leading up to the church.*

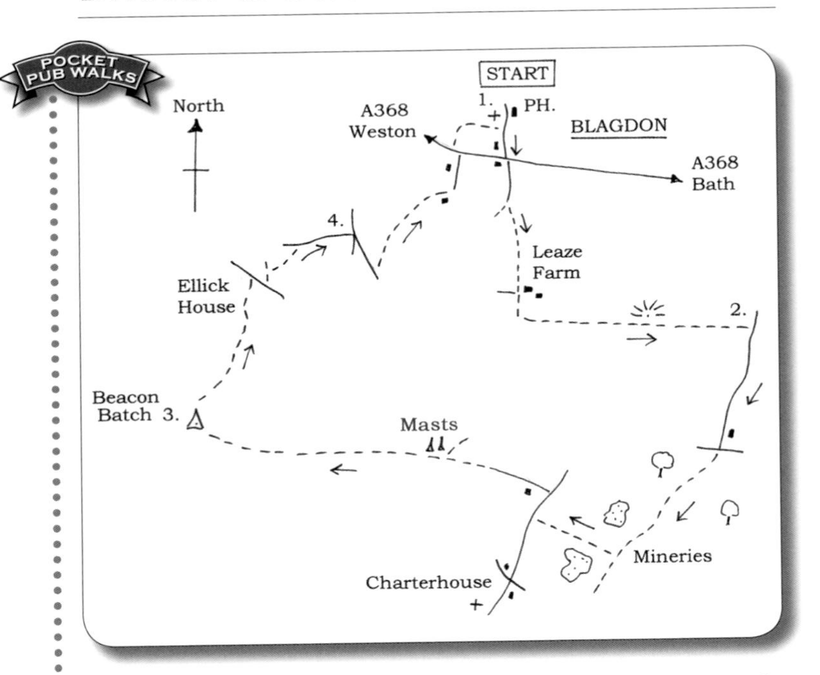

1 Walk to the A368 and follow the road opposite, Score Lane. In 250 yards, where this lane ends at a stile, continue ahead along a short section of enclosed footpath to a second stile. Cross the stile and keep ahead for 20 yards to a marker post where the path forks. Keep left, and climb out of the woodland into the corner of a hillside field. Follow the left edge of this field steeply uphill to an old stile in the top left-hand corner, before following the left edge of the following field up to a gate and a farm track. Follow the track up to a gate and lane, just beyond **Leaze Farm**. Cross this lane, and follow the green lane opposite, shown on the OS sheets as **Leaze Lane**. Keep to the green lane as it bears left in 150 yards to cross the **Mendip** hilltops. In ½ mile, pass through a hand gate and continue following the path across the left edge of an open field to a hand gate and a lane.

2 Turn right here, along **Ubley Drove**, and continue for ¾ mile to its junction with the B3134. Cross to a stile opposite and follow the right edge of the next two fields to a stile and **Nether Wood**. Ignoring all side turns, follow the path ahead for 300 yards to a marker post in the **Charterhouse mineries complex**. Turn right at this point, and follow a path that runs between a pair of former washing pools to reach a stile. Beyond this stile, follow the footpath ahead, with a boundary wall on the left-hand side, to a stile and the road leading into **Charterhouse**. Turn right along the road for 200 yards, before turning left into a cul-de-sac. Follow the lane for ½ mile to a pair of masts. Continue ahead for ½ mile along the track that passes to the left of the masts to a gateway and the open ground of **Blackdown**. Follow the well-defined track that climbs directly ahead to the trig point on **Beacon Batch**, some 600 yards distant.

3 On reaching the trig point, turn right and follow a path that drops down the hillside, heading off in a northerly direction. In 600 yards, at the bottom of the hillside, ignore all side turns at a junction and continue down the track to join the B3134

The remains of old lead workings can be seen on the walk.

alongside **Ellick House**. Turn right, cross a cattle grid, and take the first left, a driveway leading to **Lower Ellick Farm**. Just before the farmhouse, pass through a gateway on the right and follow the line of a fence on the left to a gateway. Beyond the gateway, walk diagonally across the middle of the next field to a stile in the hedgerow opposite, almost in the corner of the field. Cross the stile, turn right to a gate, and continue along a byway called **Lovers Lane** to a junction in 500 yards.

4 Take the second of two roads on the right and, in 300 yards, cross a stile on the left just before the drive leading to **Rhodyate Hill Farm**. Then follow the right edge of a field downhill to a gate in its bottom corner, fine views opening up across the **Chew Valley**. Continue downhill in a second field to a hand gate on the right, and follow a narrow enclosed footpath downhill to a property called **Seaview House**. Beyond this property, keep on the path as it bears left down to a lane. Follow this lane down to the A368; cross with care to a barrier and pavement opposite and follow the pavement to the left. In 100 yards, pass through a gateway on the right and follow a footpath down a hillside paddock to reach a tarmac path, which you follow to the right for 100 yards, to **Blagdon church**. Walk through the churchyard and continue along the lane back to **Church Street**.

Place of interest nearby

Blagdon Visitor Centre, open on Sundays from noon until 4 pm between April and August, offers a chance to go behind the scenes at Bristol Water and see what goes on to keep the water coming through your taps. See the giant Victorian beam-engine pumps and interactive displays about water, rain, reservoirs, taps and toilets, plus lots of information on the importance of water conservation. For further information, telephone Bristol Water on ☎ 0117 953 6470.

14 Axbridge

The Lamb

The Square in Axbridge is a handsome place indeed, with many attractive buildings that include the Lamb hotel, St John's church and the timber-framed house known as King John's Hunting Lodge. In the 11th century, the town had its own mint, together with a market that brought pedlars from afar to serve the needs of the Mendip farmers. It is the tops of the Mendip Hills that form our first port of call, as a stiff climb of some 600 ft brings us onto Axbridge Hill. The pain is rewarded with the gain of some quite exceptional views – to the south across Cheddar Reservoir to the Somerset Levels, and to the north across the Bristol Channel to Wales. Beyond these lofty hilltops lies the former mining centre of Shipham, where calamine was extracted in the 18th century. Quiet byways lead on to the former Yatton to Cheddar railway, often referred to as the 'Strawberry Line' on account of one of the main commodities it carried from the south-facing Mendip slopes. The line has now been transformed into a footpath and cycle route and makes for a grand finale to this delightful Mendip meander.

THE PUB The **Lamb** is a handsome three-storey whitewashed hostelry, whose flower troughs and hanging baskets add a charming touch of colour to the Square in Axbridge. With its heavy beams and open fires, cushioned wall seats and settles, there is a real feeling of tradition and history about this centuries-old inn. The reasonably priced food ranges from sandwiches and baguettes to lamb shank and duck cassoulet, whilst the real ales might include Butcombe Bitter and Gold. If you can secure one of the tables at the front of the Lamb overlooking the Square and King John's Hunting Lodge, it is quite the perfect spot to just watch the world go by.

Opening hours are 11.30 am to 3 pm and 6 pm to 11 pm; Saturday, 11.30 am to 11 pm; Sunday, noon to 10.30 pm.
☎ *01934 732253*

Distance 6½ miles

OS Explorer 141 Cheddar Gorge and Mendip Hills West. GR 431545.

A stiff climb onto Axbridge Hill, followed by more gentle walking

Starting point The Lamb at Axbridge

How to get there *Axbridge lies 2 miles west of Cheddar, on the A371 Weston-super-Mare road. Follow the signs into the town centre and turn into Moorland Street, opposite the Lamb to find one of two public car parks.*

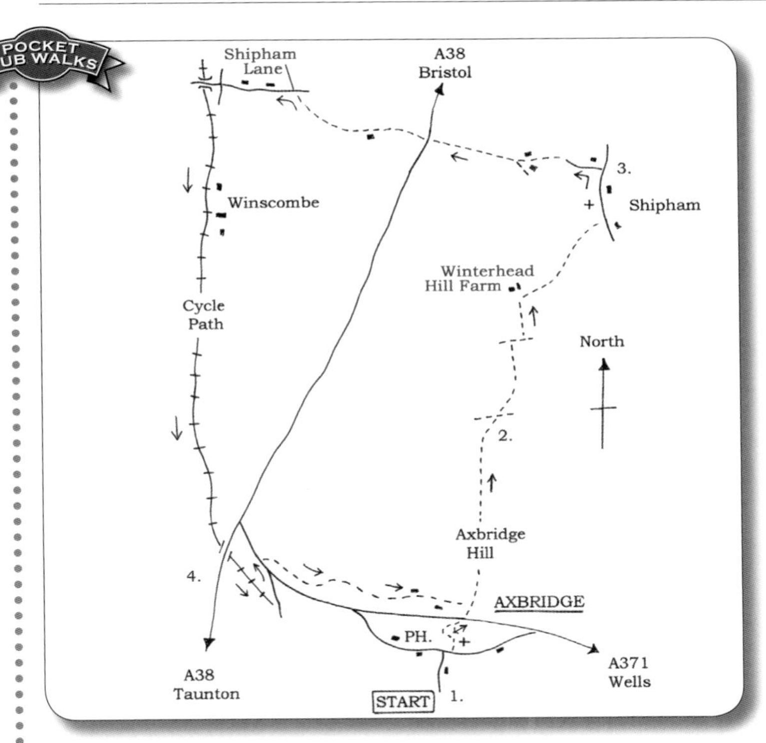

1 Walk to the eastern end of the Square in **Axbridge** and climb the steps towards the church. Rather than making for the church itself, follow a tarmac path that runs to the left of the churchyard. Just after the path bears left towards the bypass, climb some steps on the right and follow a path towards former Axbridge station, now a community centre. Opposite a netball court, cross the main road to a footpath and head uphill for 100 yards to a junction in front of a property called **Overlake**. Turn right and follow a track uphill for 250 yards to a junction of paths. Pass through the gate directly ahead and follow a footpath running steeply uphill alongside some electricity lines. In 350 yards, cross a stile in the boundary fence on the right, turn left, and continue walking uphill, the boundary now on the left. The path emerges onto the open hilltop. With the boundary on the left, keep walking ahead to a stile in the top corner of the field. Then follow the left edge of the next field to a stile in the corner. In the next field, bear half right to a gap in the wall, by a marker post one third of the way along the opposite boundary.

The Yatton to Cheddar railway line is now used as a footpath and cycleway.

2 Cross a green lane, **Callow Drove**, to a stile opposite and, in the next field, bear half right to join a sunken track just before a water trough. Follow the track downhill for 250 yards before following the left edge of an open field to a stile and **Winscombe Drove**. Turn right and, in 100 yards, go left along the drive leading to **Winterhead Hill Farm**. In 150 yards, just before the farm outbuildings, cross a stile on the right and follow a field path to a stile opposite. Cross the stile and follow the left edge of the next field to its corner before dropping down a steep, stepped path to cross a footbridge in a dip. Beyond the bridge, follow a path that climbs steeply to the left, out of the valley to a stile; then follow the left edge of the next field to a stile and a busy road. Turn left and follow the road into **Shipham**. In 300 yards, having passed the **Miners Arms**, turn left into **Comrade Avenue**.

3 At the bottom of this road, keep ahead across some grass to an old hand gate and a junction with an enclosed path. Turn right and, in 25 yards, go left at the next junction. In 300 yards, at a junction just past **Winterhead House**, turn right and follow a byway down to the A38. Cross with care and follow an enclosed track opposite. In 200 yards, where this track bears left into a property, keep ahead along a narrow footpath that runs down to a stile and open field. Walk across the field to a stile in the far right corner and continue down an enclosed path to join **Shipham Lane**. Turn left and follow this lane for ½ mile to a junction in **Winscombe**. Follow the lane opposite, **Ilex Lane**, for 75 yards to a railway bridge. Cross this bridge, turn left through an access point to the cyclepath, and drop down to the former trackbed. Follow this path to the right, away from the bridge, for 1¾ miles until it reaches the A38.

4 Cross the road with care and continue along the path opposite for 400 yards until it reaches a road just before a parking area. Turn left to the A371; follow the verge to the left for 30 yards before crossing to a footpath and gateway opposite, at the entrance to the National Trust **Shute Shelve Hill** property. Follow the grassy path across the bottom edge of the hillside to a gate and stile, before following a path through some allotments down to a junction. Turn left and follow this path to a gate and lane and some properties. At the next junction, in 175 yards, turn left and follow a byway uphill for 200 yards to a junction by a property called **Overlake**. It is now a question of turning right, down to the main road, and retracing your steps along the path behind the old station opposite, back into **Axbridge**.

Place of interest nearby

Cheddar, with its show caves and gorge, lies just a couple of miles east of Axbridge. There is also a museum that illustrates the history of the ancient peoples who settled in the area in the Stone Age. For more details on Cheddar Gorge and the Caves, ☎ 01934 742343 or visit http://www.cheddarcaves.co.uk.

15 Clevedon

The Moon & Sixpence

The sea, with its ebb and flow of tides, has long held a fascination and delight for everyone from the youngest toddler to the aged octogenarian. This quite delightful walk includes a section of the coastal path that runs between Portishead and Clevedon, bordering the Bristol Channel, a path that provides extensive views westwards towards the South Wales coast and the more distant Welsh hills. Before reaching the sea, however, a low range of hills is followed north-eastwards out of Clevedon, taking in both Castle Hill with its 17th-century folly, now a private residence, and Walton Down, with its ancient field systems and enclosures. There is also the Victorian resort of Clevedon itself, whose grey villas line the hillside above the pebble beach. The centrepiece of the town's seafront is the magnificent Victorian pier, a structure that caught the eye of none other than John